A Heartthology

**Collection of
Writings with Love**

Mackenzie,
you are loved!

Lorrine Patterson ♥

6/22/24

Table of Contents

To my Writer's Way Family and the amazing writers that inspire me every day.

Thank you for being my guiding light to writing.

To all the youth in the world, you can and will do everything your heart desires.

Never give up on you and never give up on what you love doing.

Preface

Ellis B. Leo

Do you mean it when you say, "I love you"? Whether it's to a partner, your parents, family member or friend. Do you mean it when you use the word love?

Because I do... I didn't always but now I do. Every single time I say it, I mean it. It's not a passing phrase when I say the words "I love you". Perhaps, it's because I only learnt the meaning of love very late in my life. But now I know what it is, I treasure love! I savor Love. I appreciate Love. How did I do it? First, I learnt to love myself, then I learnt to love everyone else. It's a lot harder than you think but absolutely worth it when you figure it out...

If you haven't figured it out yet, I can show you what love is; through my words and unforgettable rhythm of poetry and prose, I'll show you. Once I've shown you, I only ask you do one thing, for yourself first and then everyone else... PASS IT ON!

The Love Of Three Words

In this section, three words are added onto
each piece to create 14 poems

Grace Is

Amazing grace is….

His Hands

Outstanding, Beautiful, Elegant his hands were….

Beautiful Creativity

Creativity is not what she had, but she did....

Eyes Gaze Always

Inspiration, serenity, euphoria, the feelings I have as my eyes gaze away....

A Four-Letter Word

Love, a four-letter word yet an infinity of feelings, find it, become peacefully whole.

Transformed Into A Butterfly

Transformation, wings brightly colored seen by the unseen, orange, black and white, floating delicately through the air above.

Never-ending Dream

Transparency, foggy, blurry, confusing. She woke up from a dream she knew all too well. Could it be? Another broken heart....

Core Of My Soul

Anger, why do you hate me? I did everything you asked of me. My heart stripped with knives to the core of my soul.

The River

A River, so tranquil and calm. The rocks all have a different shape, just like the human soul. Unique in its own way. Flowing freely in me.

Empowered

Empowerment, the day I decided to take back my life. You see, I lost my way, could not conceive happiness. Darkness was my days and nights, then radiance and glow.

A Yellow Flower

Hope, believing that something greater is going to happen. A crack in the road, sun shining down upon one beautiful yellow flower. How did you grow? She whispered, Beautiful souls appear whole, complete.

A Soulful Dancer

Elevation. She jumps on her toes and glides across the newly polished floor. Spotlights shine down upon her delicate soul. Turns and twists floating effortlessly about. Her body is one with the music. Angelic, pure, flawless.

Do You Believe In Happiness?

Decide what it will take to be happy. Ask yourself this question. What do I need to change in my life to live the life I love? A need to believe you can achieve happiness, love, joy, and abundance.

Knowing Faith

Faith is knowing. Knowing that even in your darkest days, there is light despite the fight. Believe in the light. Trust in the process. Hope for the best. Be insightful. The light at the end of the tunnel is you. You are healed.

Love Fosters All

Musically inspired pieces of contemporary love

Everlasting Love Has Awakened

Everlasting as the sun, moon, and stars. I sit under the bright moon and look up at the bright stars. My heart is full and bursting with joy. Love has awakened. Tears stream down my face as I remember where I came from. A perfect place of love. My mother's womb.

My Heart Is Full of Love

I love the way your hands caress me. Soft and gentle,
my soul is smiling. My heart is full. I am whole and
complete. Your love keeps me going. I am strong because
I know that your love will guide me to the end of time.

A Journey To Eternal Love

Seems like an eternity when I started on this journey. What journey is this? A journey of pain. Not the pain in my body. Pain in my heart. It hurts. It is a pain that I can't describe. Why, oh why, do I feel this way? Please take it away. Take it away and throw it in the bay. You don't get me. Seems like an eternity since I started this journey. This journey of love.

I Am Victorious

I am victorious! I am at the top of the highest mountain screaming "I love me." I could see. See the beauty in the belief. The belief to feel the unthinkable. The unthinkable no more. It is me. The one I love the most.

Elegant Lady In Blue

Across the dance floor, he sees her, all by herself. Beautiful and elegant in her sapphire blue lace dress. Her hair is so soft and flowing. Her soft lips are red with gloss. Then suddenly, she sees him. They lock eyes as she walks towards him. He can feel her angelic energy pierce his soul. She approaches him and says, "where have you been all my life?"

Being Noble

I can't read a book. The words do not stick. I can't comprehend, so I put the book down.

Alive And Thriving in Wonder

Every day, I wake up in amazing wonderment. Life is beautiful, and I am blessed to be alive. Alive and thriving in this beautiful world. A world full of love.

Orbiting Around The World

Sunshine on my face. The warm rays feel so good, like a beautiful pink rose petal gently touching my delicate face. My heart is beaming with glee. I am thee. The higher version of myself orbiting around the world in amazement.

Romancing The Soul

I love everything about the word romance. I want to be romanced. Not just with opening a car door, but with the 24-dozen long stem red roses and a bottle of champagne waiting for me when I arrive home from a long day. I want the romance you not only feel with your hands but the kind you feel in your soul. Not that soul romance... nothing compares to the feeling of being so deeply loved by you.

Darkness Fades and Dreams Begin

I wake up to the sounds of the songbirds and bright,
warm sunshine every day. My heart is full of love and my
soul pure. I am grateful for the courage and strength to
believe that the future was bright. The darkness fades as I
wake up from the bad dreams that no longer exist.

Serene Peace At Last

Have you ever craved that feeling of peace? The feeling
of not being troubled in the mind. Chaos and toxicity are
all you know, but then, one day just like that... Serenity.

Poetic Realms in Love

Inspired by different styles of poetry

Rhyme:
Journey To Peace And Love

Peace is what I needed to release the increase of sadness
I felt.
I couldn't enjoy the joy of life.
Through my difficult experiences, I was able to build up
the resilience of having the perseverance to keep going. I
decided to live a life of gratitude with a positive attitude.
My happiness was no longer an option and became a priority.
Raspiness and snazziness put a skip in my jazziness.
Above all, love became my beautiful white dove, where I
survived the drug of love.

Pun:
Love To Sing And Dance

I would love to dance in France and sing a song by chance.
I would leave my home in California and pack my snacks
don't forget the Mac.
I would make a stop in Spain so that I won't suffer in vain
from the strain of the plane.
I would love to make more stops. Brazen it out in Brazil
and prettily dressed in Italy, but I can't forget to bet in
Tibet. I would love to dance in France and sing a song by chance.

Never give up on your dreams because they will beam
and deem your soul with ease.

Narrative:
Love Overcomes All

Have you heard of the story of how sadness found love
and light?
Sadness grew up in a home without love and carried this
throughout her life, making bad decisions along the way.
She invited over anger to dinner and asked for happiness,
courage, wisdom, love and light to come.
The first to arrive was anger. Anger was very upset at
having to come over for dinner and didn't see the point.
Courage and wisdom arrived at the same time. When they
arrived, they gave anger a hug.
Within minutes, love and light showed up and gave anger
a hug.
By the time we all sat down for dinner, anger was no
longer upset.
Anger said courage and wisdom showed me love and light.
I am no longer sad or angry.
Love overcomes all.

Nocturnal:
Stray Cats Come Out At Night

As day turns to night
The cats come out to fight
The neighbor's kindness fades away, and food becomes a
delicacy
Oh, look, there comes Stray Cat Sally. Her blue eyes send
chills up your spine as she struts her stuff down the dark
street. You can see her a mile away.
Stray Cat Howard loves Sally, but she has her eyes on
Stray Cat Tommy
Tommy has that soft white and gray fur that puts a pep in
her step
Stray cats walk the streets at night
As day turns to night and despite the fight,
The light becomes bright. There is no more appetite.

Epics:
Agape Love

Across the Mediterranean Sea,
Deep in the forest of tall trees on the highest mountain
in Greece,
Lived a little goddess
Her name was Agape
She was born with half of her heart and her parents,
Aphrodite and Apollo, loved her with all of their Heart
They both knew that one day Agape would do great
things in the world
As Agape grew older, she soon discovered her loving
heart was disintegrating slowly
Cronus, the Titan God of time, told Agape she doesn't
have much time to live and that she would soon die
before the age of 21
That day Agape received the news, she ran home crying.
Her heart is in so much pain.
She asked her parents, Why me? Why is this happening to me?

Her mother Aphrodite placed both her hands on Agape's
face and said you are meant to live this life so that you
can inspire others to keep going.

The love you have in your heart will show others that
they, too, can love beyond all the pain.

Agape wiped her tears away and from then on, she vowed to love everyone unconditionally until it was her time to transition.

Agape lived to be 111.

She transitioned into her next life with a heart full of love.

Ballad:
We Are One

Come one, Come all
We are all unique and Angelique here on the streets
You are free, love
Just like a mourning dove
Lady Love with a boxing glove
Let's stop the violence and act in anti-violence
You are not alone
Just remember to baritone,
Your precious stone
On a speakerphone

Riddle:
The Highest Vibration

I come in silent tones that can succumb to your every woe
I live beneath the skin and can feel deep within
I feel every emotion just like the deep blue ocean
I live life in the highest vibration, just like a beautiful
Hawaii vacation
What Am I?

Pastoral Poetry:
Love Is Rose

The year is 1989, a time when I didn't know the divine
At first, it was for him and would give him a limb
Forward to the year 2020
Along came a bully
I didn't know what would come next
She gifted me the ability to see a pathway of light
The pathway to my soul's evolution
As I opened my door, the sun was shining
Birds singing, bringing me the peace that I deserve in my
soul
There she was in the middle of the sun's reflection
The most beautiful hummingbird with a redneck was
coming towards me in full effect
Like a Phoenix rising from the burning ashes,
Ascension
I am whole and complete
Born again

Free Verse:
I See You Now

Born into a world without vision,
No end in sight
I never knew the fight
The fight I had in me
to see the light
The only thing I saw was the darkness
Every tear that fell from my cheek
The pain I had in my heart
was all that I felt
until one day I knelt down
Bowed my head
as I sank into my hands and said
"If Love is out there, let me see this now."
A beautiful golden image appeared
The most beautiful image that I could feel right down to
the core of my soul
I can see now
I see you
You are love,
Love is you

A Dialogue in Love

Inspired by the creativity of conversation

Welcome Home Love

"Do you feel it, Hope?"

"Feel what Faith?"

"Come on, don't mess with me,

I'm the Queen Bee."

"I'm not messing with you."

"Close your eyes

and visualize to symbolize."

"I still don't understand, Faith."

Have you taken your meds today....? hahaha."

"This is not a joking matter, Hope."

"Well then, stop being so thought-provoking

and just tell me what I'm supposed to feel, Faith."

'Well, that's exactly it.

It's not how you're supposed to feel,

it's your feelings and you could feel any way you desire.

Just remember one thing,

the next time your doorbell rings,

open the door and say,

Welcome Home Love."

The One

"You can sit here Beowulf."

"Why thank you, Songbird."

"What ya eatin' today, Beowulf?"

Ah, my mama made me my favorite lunch today. A peanut butter and jelly sandwich, with a bag of Doritos."

"That sounds delicious!"

"What ya eatin' today, Songbird?"

"My Nana made me a chicken Cesar wrap, with a bag of carrots, a side of ranch dressing, and a piece of chocolate cake for dessert."

"Wow, Songbird, that sounds amazing!"

"Thanks, Beowulf! I'm happy to share with you if you like."

"You are so kind, Songbird."

"Thanks, I try. And I believe sharing is caring."

"Well, what else do you want to share with me?"

"Since you're asking, Beowulf. I would like to share a story about the birds and the bees."

"Ok, sounds interesting."

"It actually is…. You see, there is no birds and bees' story. Just love the one you're with and be respectful to each other."

"Wow! You are so smart, Songbird. Will you be my one?"

"Yes, I will."

You Are

"Zuri, why did this happen to me?
I reflect back on my life
And don't understand why
I went through all of those hardships."
"Sarabi, my sweet girl.
Sometimes in life, we don't understand why we
experience what we experience.
When you are in the moment, it may seem like there is no
way out and you may feel like you want to disappear.
But what lies ahead of you is a life you are meant to live."
"Zuri, you always make me feel better and provide so
much clarity in my life.
As I watch this beautiful sunset with you,
I am humbled and enlightened."
"Sarabi, this is all I ever wanted for you.
Always remember that you were born for a purpose, and
your purpose is to live a life in limitless love, light, and joy.
Become who you were created to be.
Look at the world through the lens of love and focus on
your inner light.
You are the Universe.
You are Love.
You are Light"

Ascending Into Love
Inspired by Affirmations

I Am Love

I grew up in a home without love
That drove me to be a dove
Not the bird
Let's examine the word
I am Peace
I am Grace
Purity and Destiny
Brought me Hope
Hope to love again
Because Love is in the human soul
And this soul of love will never die
I am Love

I Am A Leader

I know I look different from you,
but that doesn't mean I don't deserve what is due.
My skill set is exceptional and my mind is unique,
this promotion is mine, and mine to keep.
Watch out for this girl because she can't be stopped,
her steps are extravagant, an advocate for self.
You can do anything,
believe in yourself.
When that job surfaces, just say,
I have a purpose, not fear.
I am a leader

What Is Money?

What is money?
Money is my friend.
Money is a transfer of energy from me to you.
I love money.
Money comes easily to me, and I repeat this in three.
I love money, and money loves me.
I love money, and money loves me.
I love money, and money loves me.

I Love Me

Have you heard of self-love?
Love didn't exist until I discovered how to love myself
It is the love that starts with you
You and only you can feel this
No one can make you feel this love
Self-love is the best kind of love
It is a soulful love
Beautiful to the core of your soul
Once you love yourself, everything else falls into place
Divine timing of love
I Love Me

I Am FREE

I am not me

Married at 17

I did not know that this man would be my sorrow

Love was all that I was looking for in all of my
tomorrows

9 years of mental abuse

I could now get away from the excuse

Released from this mental prison

Forgiven and risen

I am free with a guarantee to just be

Happily Ever After

Not one or two
And even three
It took four times
To read between the lines
It was like committing crimes with dimes
I found the courage to keep going
To not give up on love, but most of all, not give up on me
In 2017, I met the love of my life
He is my one true soul mate
And it all started with one date
I am Love

I Will Shine My Light

I hear stories that make me sad
They have taken another soul
I bow my head and pray
Pray for the healing
Pray for the souls that lost their loved ones
Pray for the mental health of the people
I am not going to accept this world as it is
Because as it is, is not my world
My world is bright
I am going to shine my light because my future's so bright

You Are One Of A Kind

You are smart
You are beautiful
You are loved
You are brave
You are successful
You are worthy
You are valuable
You are one of a kind

Dear Future Self

Inspired by word architecture

Love Will Lead The Way

Dear Lorrine,

Wow! Look at you now!! You are an amazing best-selling Author, International Podcast Host, Worldwide Speaker and Founder/CEO of a nonprofit!! If you think that the doors of opportunity and abundance stopped there, you are more of an inspiration to the world with your new tv show streaming on Netflix, Hulu, Amazon Prime and many, many more platforms. You have also joined a successful production organization as an Executive Director and are doing amazing things, changing lives, one heart at a time. You continue to further your education and collaborate with many people who will guide and support you. Your world is full of abundance, joy, happiness, success and love. I see your future and your future is bright because you continue to shine your light no matter what obstacles have come your way. Continue to lead in love. Be that guiding light that you were meant to be. Keep inspiring the world through your encouragement and message. You are the Universe!

Your Health is Your Wealth

Dear Lorrine,

You have been through so much in your life and have come so far! 33 years ago, you wanted to disappear. Disappear from this world. The only world you knew. You wanted to go to a world of love and remove the pain in your soul. You worked hard for the last 33 years to remove the pain. The pain with no gain. Remove the hazardous waste that you never wanted to taste. Toxicity was no longer a part of your life. You found the love that you are worthy of. You are healthy in your mind, body and soul. Your health is your wealth, and no one will ever take that from you…. period.

Love Always Wins

Dear Lorrine,

Love has not always been your greatest strength. In fact, you had so much love to give and was giving it to the wrong people. People who didn't deserve the love you had, but you did it anyway. Mostly because you were not taught how to love or what love is. As years went on, you were lost and confused. Jumping from one relationship to the next, hoping and wishing that this would be the one. Until you finally after 29 years of searching, realized that the greatest love of all was inside of you. You found self-love. The truest form of love was inside of you all of your life. You may not have had love all of your life, but what counts is the love that you found within you. You are loved. Love is You. Love always wins!

Ascending Into Greatness

Dear Lorrine,

2020 was the year of ascension. You joined a creative virtual writing workshop for fun. The writing prompts brought out the best in you. A creativity you never knew you had. A skill set that seemed to be unreachable. You sat down with your laptop and started writing your book. Doubt settled in. Who are you to write a book? Despite all your fears and doubts, you completed your manuscript at the end of 2020 and published your first book, Freeing Your Heart For Love in April 2021. You knew that your mission and passion were to do more. What is beyond the book? You launched a podcast show, became a public speaker sharing your story to inspire others, started a nonprofit to help teenage girls challenged with abuse and depression and will launch your own tv TV show in 2022. You finally discovered your purpose. Life is amazing, and you are blessed. You will do amazing things in the years to come. This is only the
beginning. You are ascending into greatness!

Note Full of Love

Inspired by music

Respect Is

Why do you stand there and act like I don't mean
anything?

Do you understand my power within?

Your pride and ego do not impress me

All it does is frees me and spins me

To do a dropkick and whip around

with a sound that is world-renowned

Everyone deserves respect

Respect is not earned

Respect is valued

Respect is what we need to come together

Respect is Love

Through The Darkness, There is Light

We are born with the innocence of pure love
The love that we all have in our hearts
Our youth is guided to a place
A place of love, forgiveness, healing, joy and happiness
Let's Live and Heal
The world can be a better place
It starts with us
Let's all come together and heal mother earth
Through our Love and Light
Hold that light close to you and don't let go
The light will get us through the darkness
It all starts with you

The Power is Within You

My beautiful love
You help me to see the sun and moon
Stars sparkling in my eyes
The green trees and yellow flowers are vibrant
The ocean waves ripples in my heart
My soul is filled with soft rose petals
Dropping delicately in my body
Don't ever forget
The power is within you

Let's Dance

Let's Dance
I get my kicks with my hips and tricks
Oh the quickstep is not a thing
Just bop beep and peep
Back and forth yakety-yak
Like a girl on Broadway in a jazz lounge
Cigar in one hand
Whiskey in the other
Piano playing to the tunes of my soul
The trumpet is in my bones
To the core of my legs
Let's Dance and prance

Opportunity And Unity

Unity and Opportunity
Disrespect and deflect
Rock bottom gave me a chance with a stance
You don't deserve this beautiful soul
Ego has got to go
Walk on until you come upon
Respect and then redirect
Your attention to reconnect

Red Heels Sings The Blues

Strutting down the street in red heels
Whistling to BB King who is singing the blues
The blues is what gives me the clues
Clues to who this mystery woman is in the red high heels
What is that paper in her hands?
The deed to my soul
She can have my soul
Her love so deep
I sing the blues to the tunes of her heartbeat
Whistling turns to howling
Howl at me
Growl at me
Sing the blues to me
You are my Queen
I am your King

With This Heart, I do

Today, I open my heart and profess my love to you
My heart is open to you
Love lives here
Welcome into my world
This world won't let you down
I am full of love
The light of love will guide us
To a place of magical love
Filled with hope, inspiration and joy
I will show you the way
Walk with me hand in hand
Place your heart in my hands
With this heart, I vow to love you
I promise to take care of you
Until the end of my days and nights
With this heart, I do
I do love you

Worry No More

What do you want to do?
Do you want to cha cha cha?
Grab my hand
Let's Go
We will release all of your worries
One cha-cha at a time
Catch my breath
As we dance the night away
Your glow shining brightly
For the world to see
Don't let anyone worry you
Pretty minds marry me

Decades of Love

Inspired by different decades

Broken And Mended

"The world breaks everyone and afterward many are strong at the broken places."
~Ernest Hemmingway

Many come from broken places
Broken places come with pieces
Pieces that can be mended
Pretending and defending
To be someone you are not
To fit into a crowd
That frowns and puts down
You never gave up
You rose up and picked up the broken pieces of your delicate heart
You mended these pieces with your fragile hands and gave healing to a friend
You are healed
You are strong and not a daylong overdue
Broken places and pieces can be mended

A Tribute To Louis Armstrong

"My whole life, my whole soul, my whole spirit is to blow that horn,"~ Louis Armstrong

Life is like jazz
Tuning in to the rhythm of the light
A trumpeter with a flair
Developing jazz into fine art
The first great jazz soloist
An entertainer loved by many
A hero of triumph and positivity
Devotion to his music
Satchmo, I will forever miss you
Blissed in this wonderful world

Blue Eyes

"The best gift you can give yourself is the gift of possibility."~ Paul Newman

Blue eyes so deep
Not just an actor with good looks
A philanthropist with a giving heart
You may know him from the delicious sauces
That warm your belly and are food to the soul
His motto, "Let's give it all away to those who need it."
100% of profits are given to charities
A passionate race-car driver with a heart of gold
Blue eyes will mesmerize

Luck Of A Bright Star

"No matter who you are, no matter what you did, no matter where you've come from, you can always change, become a better version of yourself." ~ Madonna

A lucky star released from a jar
Plucked from the universe, not a curse
Bright light in the world swirled in pearls
My name, who overcame
Prayer does not compare
Love will lead the way
Dancing to the tunes
Dressed up in your love
Material girls living their best life
In this material world
Queen of Pop
We won't stop
Becoming who we are meant to be

Kobe The Great

The most important thing is to try and inspire people so
that they can be great in whatever they want to do.

~ Kobe Bryant

Gone too Soon
NBA Hall of Famer
One of the greatest players in this generation
50 shots in one game brought the fame to his flame
A writer, singer, and legend
Mamba Mentality lives on
Your time here will never be forgotten
Ti vogliamo bene

The Will To Survive

"What separates us from the animals, what separates
us from the chaos, is our ability to mourn people we've
never met." ~ David Levithan

September 11, 2001
A day we will never forget
It would change our world
People we never met
Families lost
Trapped and rescued
The will to survive
A lifetime to not feel alive
Why did you take my mom?
Why did you take my dad?
Why did you take my friend?
Why did you take my sister?
Why did you take my brother?
Resilience and Hope
Love and Honor
Will continue to live on

Rise Up

"We realize the importance of our voices only when we are silenced."~ Malala Yousafzai

It only takes one person
One person to have a voice
For the voices unheard
The voices suppressed from shame and fear
Three shots didn't stop her
Continued threats were fuel for her mission
A Nobel Prize Winner
A women's rights and education activist
Advocates Rise Up

Mother Love

"I'm proud of many things, but nothing beats that of being a mother."~ Unknown

18 years old
Blooming from the new seeds
I lost hope and Love
Confusion and depression were my days and nights
Motherhood saved me from the next life
Love of my boys
Bring me joy
Mind, body, and soul
My heart is whole

Journey Behind the Author

Never Too Late For Anything

My writing journey started in 2020. Did I always want to be a writer? No, it was something that happened to me at the right time in my life. A new love and passion inside of me that I never knew I had until I met and surrounded myself with incredible people who helped me to understand this new passion and purpose in life. Everything that I went through in my life made sense when I started writing. Let me take you back to the beginning and share a bit about how I discovered my purpose as a writer and author.

Growing up in a home full of chaos and disfunction was something I could never understand. A home without love and warmth. I never knew what love felt like. What it felt like to be hugged by my parents and to hear those three precious words, I love you. I never heard my parents tell me that they are proud of me or that I will grow up to be a successful and amazing person. I never heard the laughter of my siblings in the other room. All that I heard was yelling and silence. Yelling when my mom or dad would tell us to do something. Silence when I was left home alone to care for myself. The silence after I was yelled at and could only hear the faint sobbing that came from my heart and tears that fell down my cheek.

As I grew older, I attracted more unloving people into my life. I wasn't aware of what I was doing because no one taught me how to love or how to be loved. I yearned to feel love and wanted to love someone with all my heart and soul. I continually gave my heart and soul to the wrong people. People who took advantage of my already weakened heart, but I would still try to make them love me. I would do things that only made me feel more unloved. I started slipping into a downward spiral of feeling depressed and suicidal. I prayed and searched for peace and love. Peace in my soul and love in my heart. I saw therapists, read self-help books and talked to anyone who would listen.

It took me 29 years to discover my happiness and self-love. My writing journey started when I was ready to share my story with the world. My entire life, I was searching for other people to love me when the one person who needed to love me was myself. The power of self-love. Once I started loving myself, all of the unloving and abusive people started to disappear from my life. I started building healthy relationships and met people who loved me for who I was. I didn't have to pretend to be someone so that they would love me.

This book was an Anthology idea brought together
by a group of amazing writers from all over the world
who met on an app called Clubhouse. Strangers who
are now family. The Writer's Way Family. Although the
Anthology didn't get published, I learned different styles
of writing and was able to open up my mind to more
creativity that was locked up inside of me. I realized
that the writer in me was always there. I didn't have
the environment, encouragement and support I needed
to unlock this part of my mind. I just needed to find
the key to unlock this part of my mind and I found it
by surrounding myself with supportive, creative "write
minded" people.

I am not here to tell you my life is perfect, and I still
have those days when doubt enters my mind, but I think
about how far I have come and always find my way
back. My way back to love and me. I even have a love
symbol that helps me to remember how loved I am. The
hummingbird. When I open the blinds to my backyard,
a hummingbird appears to remind me of love and at that
moment, I know that I will always be ok and so will you.